The English Bible and Its Origins

RICHARD PURKIS

First published by Shuter and Shooter, South Africa, 1978.

Second Edition published by Angel Press,
PO Box 60, Chichester, West Sussex, PO20 8RA.

British Library Cataloguing in Publication Data

Purkis, Richard
The English Bible and its origins.—2nd ed.
1. Bible—History
I. Title II. Bible beginnings
220'.09 BS445

ISBN 0-947785-23-X

Typeset in Times by Woodfield Graphics, Fontwell, West Sussex.
Printed in Great Britain.

CONTENTS

Acknowledgements

The cover photograph is reproduced by courtesy of the Bible Society's Library at Cambridge University Library; the Sumerian clay tablet by permission of the British Museum; the Lachish letter by permission of the trustees of the late Sir Henry Wellcome; the view of Cave 4 by permission of BIPAC; and the view of St. Catherine's Monastery by permission of David Sutcliffe.

The Versions of Psalm 23: The Authorised Version by permission of Eyre and Spottiswoode (Publishers) Ltd; the New English Bible copyright 1970 Oxford & Cambridge University Presses, published by the Bible Societies and Collins; the Good News Bible copyright American Bible Society, used by permission; the Living Bible used by permission of Tyndale House 1971.

PART ONE

The Beginnings of the Bible

1. From Clay to Paper

> When I awoke early in the morning I went to my mother and said to her, "Give me my lunch, I have to go to school." The monitor in charge said, "You are far too late." Afraid and with pounding heart I went respectfully to my teacher. "Go to your place," he said. And then he looked at my writing and was angry and he caned me.

Sumerian cuneiform—2300 BC

You will be relieved to know that this school has since closed down—about 4000 years ago! For this story is a translation of part of a writing exercise for boys at a tablet-house (or school) only a few miles from Ur, where Abraham was to be born 100 years later. This school of about 2000 BC was called the tablet-house because all exercises were done on soft clay tablets in a system of markings we now call cuneiform (from Latin—"wedge-shaped"—see picture). The stylus used for making these impressions was probably a sharpened reed cut to a three-sided end. Writing had developed by Abraham's time from sentences made up of a series of simple pictures (called pictographs) to their replacement by groups of marks for syllables and words. Cuneiform was written from left to right.

Other languages, such as Egyptian (hieroglyphics) and Chinese, later adopted a similar method although, of course, using different symbols.

In Abraham's day, then, there was a well-developed system of writing with schools, dictionaries, and tax returns. But cuneiform has three major disadvantages:

Sumerian clay tablet (Epic of Gilgamesh)

1. It is clumsy—Sumerian cuneiform had 600 different symbols;
2. It needs to be cut into clay or stone or hardened wax and is therefore slow to write;
3. It is bulky for storage—a tablet the size of this book could only contain this chapter.
   The most important records even needed a clay envelope to protect them.

The Alphabet—1300 BC

By the time Abraham's descendents, the children of Israel, were invading Canaan under Joshua, perhaps the most important development in language was well under way—the invention of the alphabet. Instead of a group of marks (as in cuneiform) representing the sound of a complete word or syllable, each letter of the alphabet represents a single basic sound of the spoken language. The first attempt was made at Ugarit (on the Mediterranean seaboard) with an alphabet of 32 cuneiform shapes.

One of the Lachish letters

The Hebrew language uses a 22-letter alphabet. It has no vowels in it.

The early forms of the letters were sharp and angular so that they could be inscribed in clay or stone, but now it was possible to form the shapes easily with a pen or brush so that a greater variety of writing materials could be used.

From your experience of washing up at home you will know how easily pottery can break, and one very common material used for writing was broken pieces of unglazed pottery (called *ostraca* from Greek for "potsherd"). These fragments of worthless, unglazed pottery were used for making notes, receipts and even, in time of emergency, for letters.

Papyrus

With the development of the alphabet came an interest in a creamy, smooth-textured writing material called papyrus which the Egyptians had been using for centuries. The papyrus reed, which grew in the Nile, was a most useful plant. It was used for making anything from houses to fuel, from ropes and mats to boats (Moses' "ark of bulrushes" was of papyrus—Exodus 2:3). Even the leaves were made into a kind of chewing gum. To make paper (we get this word from papyrus) the pith of the reed was stripped and laid vertically edge to edge. A second layer was then placed horizontally (over the top of the first layer) the two layers being soaked and then bonded together under pressure. The surface was finally cleaned and polished and cut into suitable pieces. Writing was usually on the horizontal side since the pen would write more smoothly along the grain. Several pieces were then gummed edge to edge to form a roll of paper (scroll). The easiest way was to start at the right hand and work "backwards" in the scroll. Hebrew is still written from right to left. By 1100 BC (100 years before David became king) we read of the King of Byblos (in Lebanon) importing 500 scrolls of fine quality papyrus from Egypt in exchange for a consignment of timber.

Byblos in fact became a famous centre for trading in papyrus. So much so that the Greeks began to call a papyrus scroll a *biblion* (from Byblos) and a set of scrolls *biblia* from which we get our word Bible. For, remember, the Bible is not just one book but a collection, a library of books. The 39 books of the Old Testament were mainly in Hebrew, one of the earliest languages in the world to use an alphabet.

Aramaic—1000 BC

If you look at the map of the development of writing (page 6) you will see that Israel and its Canaanite neighbours, were not the only peoples to develop an alphabet. To the North East lay the growing powers of Aram (Syria) and Assyria and their language, Aramaic. This was destined to become the major language of the Middle East. The Persians adopted Aramaic as the official tongue for their wide-flung empire, stretching from Pakistan to Greece. It is not surprising, therefore, that parts of the Old Testament were originally in Aramaic (note especially Ezra 4:8; 6:18; 7:12–26 and Daniel 2:4—7:28). To summarise our findings so far:

1. Written language began in the Middle East:
   (a) as pictures of actual objects or people (pictographs—eg. early Sumerian, and Egyptian Hieroglyphics)
   (b) as signs or symbols representing words and syllables (cuneiform, about 2500 BC) and hieractic Egyptian)
   (c) as single letters (alphabet) for each distinctive sound of a language. (e.g. Ugaritic cuneiform, alphabetic Hebrew, about 1300 BC, and Aramic)
2. Writing materials developed parallel with the progress towards the alphabet:
   (a) carved or inscribed stone and clay or wax (cuneiform)
   (b) Papyrus (Egypt and thence to alphabet countries)
   (c) fragments of unglazed pottery (ostraca).

There were three main disadvantages with these systems of writing that had developed up to this point:

1. These early alphabets had no vowels so that sentences would look like this: THS WS MY BK
   The word "BK" could stand for "book", "beak", "bike" or even "bookie". Only the context (the rest of the passage)

The Development of Writing

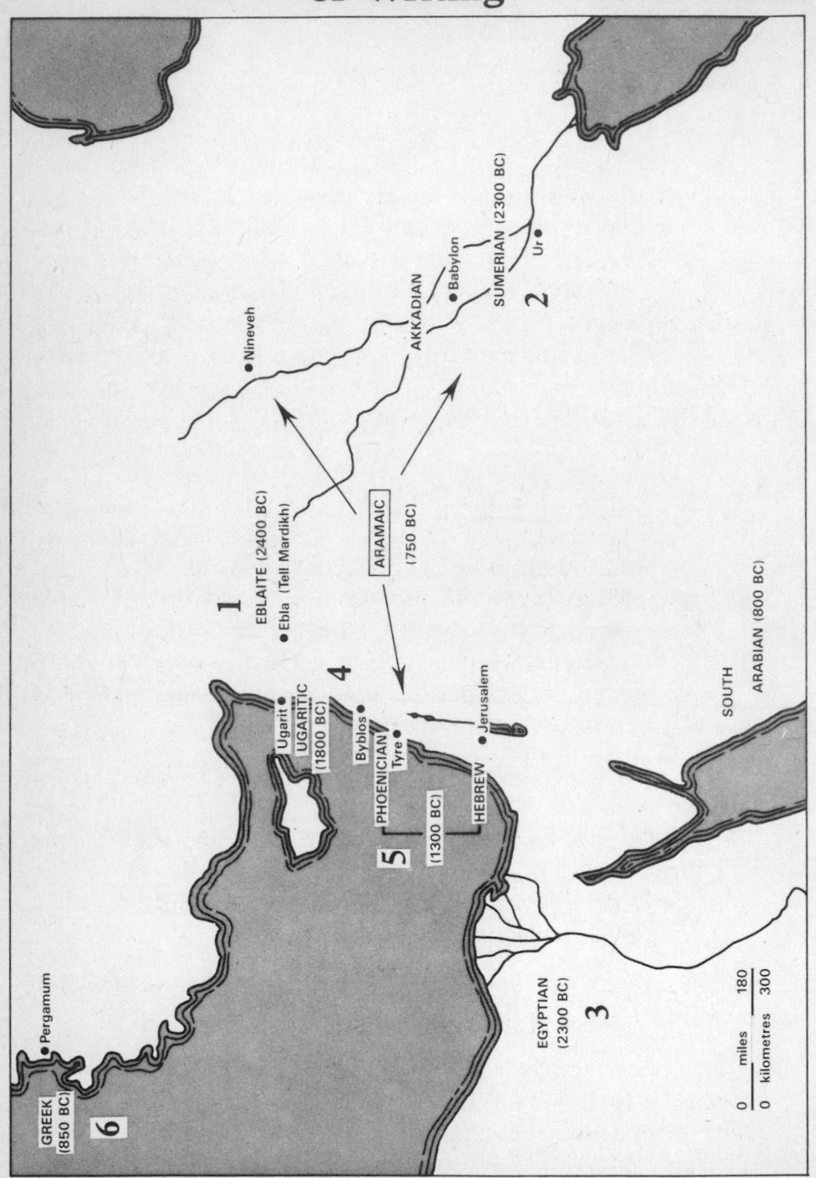

KEY TO MAP

	Approximate Dates BC
1. EBLAITE—cuneiform (i) a developed syllabic language resembling Hebrew (ii) the earliest form of Sumerian logograms (symbols = words).	2400
2. SUMERIAN—cuneiform more developed logograms—syllabic also neighbouring Akkadian.	(?) 2300 (earlier dates must now be suspect)
3. EGYPTIAN—heiroglyphic (i) the heiroglyphic symbols were first pictographic but eventually became alphabetic. (ii) demotic script (alphabetic) for the common people came very much later.	2300
4. UGARITIC—cuneiform first attempt at an alphabet (32 symbols).	1800
5. PHOENICIAN/CANAANITE first true alphabet with symbols from which our alphabet is derived. Hebrew was an early user of this method of writing	1300 (but probably earlier attempts were made)
6. GREEK first alphabet to include vowels.	850
Other language groups referred to on the map: SOUTH ARABIAN developed into modern Arabic from its beginnings (about 800 BC) as an alphabetic language. ARAMAIC became the international language of the Fertile Crescent with the rise of Persia.	800

Note: The Sumerians and Egyptians began to use pictographic symbols in about 3000 BC, but this is not true writing.

where the sentence was found could decide which was the correct meaning.

2. The new alphabets read from right to left which meant that right-handed people found writing awkward, since they tended to smudge when using ink.

3. Apart from clay tablets (not well-suited to the new alphabets) writing materials did not last long. Ostraca could easily be chipped and their odd shapes were not easy to store. Papyrus did not last long before it went brown and became flaky and readily torn.

Greek alphabet—850 BC

The Greeks tackled each of these points after adopting the idea of an alphabet from the Phoenicians about 850 BC. From the beginning they included letters for vowel sounds, often using existing Phoenician letters for which Greek had no similar sound.

The Greeks experimented with the direction of writing on the page, even trying out a system of alternative lines:

L ➧ R	Line 1
L ⬅ R	Line 2
L ➧ R	Line 3 etc.

This was called *Boustrophedon* ("As an ox ploughs"). Imagine how confusing this would be for reading. In the end they adopted the method we are used to—reading from left to right.

Parchment

In the field of writing materials, the Greeks were responsible for popularising the use of skins of sheep and goats, specially treated and far more permanent than papyrus. Just as the Greeks called scrolls of papyrus, *biblia* (after the port of Byblos) so now they referred to skins treated for writing on as *parchment* (deprived from the town in Asia Minor which was a major producer of these skins, Pergamum). Parchment, like papyrus, was only written on one side (obviously the non-hair side) and pieces were sewn, end to end, to form a scroll.

2. Latest news on early languages (Tell Mardikh)

In the spring of 1976 an archaeological discovery of tremendous importance was made in northern Syria (see map page 6-7). "It is as if we had suddenly found out about Rome and the Roman Empire," one American professor has put it. For this discovery at Tell Mardikh is opening up one of the most mysterious periods of history—the period between Noah's Flood and Abraham (Genesis 10 and 11; roughly 2400–2000 BC).

Tell Mardikh consists of a mound (parts of which have already been excavated) of 140 acres, lying about 40 miles south of Aleppo and 65 miles north-east of Damascus. It lies on a number of ancient trade routes and was clearly a very important trade centre in the 3rd millenium BC. The ancient name of this city state, which flourished before Abraham was born, was Ebla. As we shall see it had its own language, written in cuneiform script. It had a sophisticated civil service administering the district around the city and was responsible for a total regional population of 200,000. As we have already remarked, the Eblaite civilisation has been a quite remarkable discovery of the late 1970s and is still being assessed by archaeologists and historians. However, our interest in Ebla will be largely confined to its importance from the point of view of the development of language, especially Hebrew.

The Bible World-Picture—

Genesis 10 presents us with a well-populated world following the Flood, with mankind already divided into separate nations (altogether 70 are named in this chapter) covering the whole of the Fertile Crescent.

The Bible claims that something very dramatic happened within two centuries of the Flood, which caused these nations to move outward from what we now call the Middle East. Look at Genesis

10:5 for example, where the Mediterranean islands were populated, according to this record, by peoples from the mainland.

The Tower of Babel and Languages

What brought about this sudden expansion of the earth's population over a much wider area?

Genesis 11: 1–9 gives the Bible answer—the story of the Tower of Babel and the confusion of human language (note verse 9). Until 1976 most scholars dismissed this story of the sudden development of languages as fanciful and most unlikely. Now serious students of archaeology can no longer be so sure; the discoveries at Tell Mardikh have produced strong support for this Bible world-picture. Let us look at the facts that have so far come to light.

The Languages of Tell Mardikh—

1. Eblaite

Chief amongst the finds at Tell Mardikh, so far, has been the discovery of a library of 18,000 clay tablets mostly dating from

Eblaite*	Hebrew	Meaning
MA-LI-KU-UM	MALEKUTH	Kingdom
BE-HE-MOT	BEHEMOTH	wild elephant – meaning uncertain until Tell Mardikh finds. (see Job 40:15-24)
TOB	TOB	good
TA-MIN	TAMMIN	perfect

*Some scholars call Eblaite (this 'Hebrew' language on the Tell Mardikh tablets) – 'paleo-Canaanite' (ancient Canaanite)

the period 2400–2000 BC. All are written in cuneiform (the wedge-shaped writing referred to in the last chapter). But they are not all in the same language.

In fact, the majority are in a language that was not previously known to exist, and yet which bears a very strong likeness to Hebrew. This Hebrew-type language was the language spoken at Tell Mardikh (or Ebla, as the tablets call the city) long before Abraham was born. Just to show how close this language is to Hebrew, see Table for a few examples.

You may have noticed that the Eblaite words are divided into syllables. This is because this language was written in syllabic cuneiform (see page 5, 1(b)). This means that this early "Hebrew"—type language was already well-developed, even in its written form, because it had left the pictographic ('picture-writing') stage behind long ago.

The Languages of Tell Mardikh—

2. Sumerian logograms—2200 BC

The next most used language on the tablets is also a surprise, but for a different reason. Unlike Eblaite which has proved that Hebrew can be traced back much earlier than archaeologists had thought, the Sumerian tablets at Tell Mardikh cast serious doubt on the belief that Sumerian was the first written language in the world.

The Sumerian on these tablets is the most primitive (at the earliest stage of development) of this language yet found. This Sumerian cuneiform is almost pictographic (that is, each word being represented by a picture—like Hieroglyphic ≈≈≈ = water). Pure pictographic writing is very difficult in cuneiform because of the straight lines of the wedge. But in the Sumerian tablets found at Tell Mardikh each group of wedge-symbols is a word (called a logogram from Greek *logos* = word).

Logograms have limitations: there is a problem in conveying abstract ideas, but more important there are obviously hundreds of symbols to be learnt to read and write in logograms. Soon there is the need to look for symbols to represent the smaller unit of the syllable.

Yet here is a Sumerian logogram language dating from about 2200 BC. Previously archaeologists have dated the much more developed logogram-syllabic Sumerian (found in the Persian Gulf end of the Fertile Crescent) in 3100 BC. Clearly this date will have to be treated to close scrutiny.

There are further indications from Tell Mardikh that Eblaite, or paleo-Canaanite, (the ''Hebrew'' language of the tablets) is an older language than Sumerian. Amongst the tablets are bilingual items, including pronunciation dictionaries in which Eblaites were told how to pronounce Sumerian in terms of the ''Hebrew'' sounds. (Of course, this does not necessarily mean that the ''Hebrew''/Eblaite was an older language than Sumerian; it might simply be that Eblaite was the native language of Tell Mardikh and Sumerian therefore a foreign language.

The Languages of Tell Mardikh—

3. The 42-language tablets

Quite without parallel anywhere else in archaeological discovery is the existence amongst the Tell Mardikh finds of large tablets having up to 42 different languages on a single slab.

These, obviously, consist principally of word lists in the various languages. But they give us a very clear indication that, for some reason, the Eblaites took a quite extraordinary interest in languages.

Why?

The Bible and Tell Mardikh tablets

One fact must be obvious by now. At about the same time as the Bible claims that the Tower of Babel incident happened, Tell Mardikh (or Ebla to use its name at that time) became suddenly very interested in languages.

The Bible assumes that a language very like Hebrew was the original language. Names in the opening chapters of Genesis, such as Adam, Enoch, and Noah all have meanings in Hebrew but not in other early languages. The weight of evidence from Tell Mardikh points to Eblaite/Hebrew being the most advanced, and therefore earliest, of all the languages on the tablets (and this includes Sumerian which has previously been thought the oldest written language in the world.)

The tablets tell us that the King of Ebla about that time was a man named Ebrum (or Eber). A man named Eber is mentioned in Genesis 10:25 (note Eber's importance — v. 21). It was in the days of Eber's son, Peleg, that "the earth was divided," by the introduction of languages according to the Bible. Is this similarity of the name Eber on the tablets and in Genesis 10 mere coincidence?

The Bible and the Ebla (Tell Mardikh) World-picture

Perhaps even more important than this apparent evidence that Tell Mardikh provides to confirm the Bible is that it establishes, beyond any doubt, that the whole of the Fertile Crescent was highly-civilised hundreds of years before Abraham was born at the advanced city of Ur.

Ebla (the old name for Tell Mardikh) was the centre of a commercial Empire which reached to Egypt, Turkey, Mesopotamia and beyond. It had trade agreements with peoples even 2,500 kms (1600 miles) away. These treaties were reinforced by military power. Familiar names such as Jerusalem, Megiddo and Gaza occur on these tablets proving that these cities existed before Abraham came to the Land of Promise. It is most interesting that Sodom and Gomorrah and the other cities in the Dead Sea area, destroyed in Abraham's lifetime (see Genesis 14 and 19) are actually listed on the tablets.

Its laws would have delighted Women's Lib since they specifically gave women equality with men, indeed the punishments for crimes against women were most severe. Other tablets contain weather forecasts, describe a form of state socialism and refer to nationalised industries—all before 2000 BC. Ebla was probably the first free trade city in the world.

There are tablets describing the regular shipment of live fish, in salt-water tanks on river barges, right from the Persian Gulf up the Euphrates to the north.

The city of Ebla itself supported a population of about 40,000 people. Its administrative centre was protected by high limestone-slab walls, 12 metres thick at their base. This area (about 140 acres) included the Royal palace, in whose out-buildings the 18,000 clay tablets have been found. The palace has yet to be excavated,

The south gate of Ebla (Tell Mardikh)

but already is known to be a massive and impressive building. Made in terraces up the hillside that forms the centre of Ebla, its interior walls were painted grey-green and some have murals for decoration. It was about the time of King Eber (Ebla's third King according to the tablets) that this magnificent palace was begun.

Other names of people (apart from Eber) which we later find given to Bible characters, are common on the tablets and include: Abram, Jacob, Israel, David (strangely enough a name not previously known outside the Bible) and Michaiah = "who is like Yah?"

This last name brings us to our final point. The bible uses the Hebrew name *Yahweh* for God over 6,000 times in the Old

Testament (usually represented by "LORD" or "GOD" in our Bibles. Yahweh is used nearly 150 times in the book of Genesis, yet scholars have claimed that this name for God was not known or used in the Genesis period. The Ebla tablets frequently use the abbreviation "Ya" for God hundreds of years before Abraham. Tell Mardikh is clearly one of the most important archaeological finds in history.

3. The Old Testament takes shape

The Old Testament claims to reveal God communicating with man. "Thus saith the LORD," (Hebrew = Yahweh) is one of its key phrases, and what God said had to be written down.

Many different explanations of exactly how and when this written record was set down have been suggested. What follows in this chapter is the impression we get from a simple reading of the Bible as it stands. We begin with the earliest references to writing—in the book of Exodus (although the word "book" first occurs in Genesis 5:1). Moses, we are told "wrote down all the words of the Lord," when the Law was given to the Israelites at the Mount Sinai (Exodus 24:4–8). Later, just before he died, Moses gave a series of talks to the people of Israel and once again, "wrote down all this rule of life," being careful to pass on a written copy to his successor, Joshua (Exodus 17:14; Deuteronomy 31:22–29).

The Book of the Law

When Joshua reached the end of his life, he, like Moses before him, reminded the nation of their history and then went on to extract a solemn promise from the people to obey God's laws (Joshua 24:1–16). Like Moses, the aged Joshua wrote the terms of this agreement "in the book of the law" (Joshua 24:26). In this manner, book by book, the Old Testament grew.

There was a great deal written which was not finally included in the collection of books we now find in the Old Testament. Each king, for example, kept official accounts of his reign, even having a number of different biographies written about him (King David, for instance—1 Chronicles 29:29, 30). These records no longer exist, but they were available for reference by the final authors of the "God's eye view" histories of the nation that are in our Old Testament (2 Chronicles 33:18).

Ezra and the History Books

There is some evidence that a priest called Ezra was involved in compiling the history of the kingdom of Judah which we find in the Bible Books of Chronicles (note how the last verses of 2 Chronicles are identical with the opening verses of Ezra). Ezra lived about 450 BC (more than 1000 years after the death of Moses) and yet his appeal was still to the "book of the Law" which he read to his people during a special week's holiday that he had ordered to be kept (Nehemiah 8:1–8). Once again he reminded them of their history as God's people (Nehemiah 9:5–37).

And what a strange history it is. Totally unlike the boastful inscriptions of successes and conquests which make up the official histories of the surrounding nations, Israel's history speaks very critically, in the main, of Israel and her rulers. This is just what gives the Old Testament its tremendous importance. Strictly speaking it is not a history of a nation, but rather the story of how God controls history even when His people try to go it alone; it tells of how God remains faithful to His word even when those He loves are unfaithful. It makes clear the amazing fact that God can triumph in spite of our failures.

How Jeremiah's Words were Recorded

"The Book of the law" which Ezra and his fellow priests read from during that memorable week was, of course, not the original scroll, in Moses' own handwriting. These works of Moses were no doubt on fragile papyrus scrolls. There is a painful story in the book of Jeremiah which illustrates how easily a papyrus scroll could be destroyed. Jeremiah was told by God to "take a scroll and write all the words I have spoken to you about Jerusalem and Judah and all the nations from the day I first spoke to you . . . until today." (Jeremiah 36:1–16). This took several months during which the prophet dictated his message to a scribe called Baruch (compare Jeremiah 36:1 with v 9). When the long task was completed, the scroll was taken to the king who listened with growing anger to the first few columns of the scroll (not surprising when we read Jeremiah 1:14–16 and 2:26–32). Then the King "cut them off column by column with a penknife and threw them into the fire."

He went on doing so until the whole scroll had been thrown into the fire . . . Then the word of the Lord came to Jeremiah, "Now take another scroll . . . " (36:28). You can imagine Baruch's frustrated anger at having to start all over again. (Read Jeremiah 45 if you want to see how Baruch felt).

The Prophets knew their "Bibles"

And yet despite this kind of set-back we find another prophet, Daniel, (living in Babylon, 1000 kms (850 miles) away by road from Jerusalem) reading a copy of the book of Jeremiah only about seventy years later (Daniel 9:2). This brings us to a most intriguing fact. The writers of the Bible read and quoted from already existing books which had stood the test of time.

Jeremiah's favourite reading, for example, seems to have been Deuteronomy and the prophets Hosea and Isaiah. Hosea, in turn, loved delving into the book of Genesis and the early history of the nation of Israel. Several of the Psalms show a detailed knowledge of the books of Exodus and Numbers.

The straightforward evidence of the Old Testament itself, then, suggests that many of its writers were eyewitnesses of the events they describe and that the prophets in particular studied the books of earlier writers, whom they believed wrote from God.

4. The Earliest Old Testament is found

Journey to Qumran

In imagination we take a journey. We shall not be able to travel by car, or even four-wheel-drive vehicles, for our journey is also in time, back to 35 BC. Heat, like a hammerblow, smites us. We left Jerusalem (temperate, even cold) in the early morning and took the notorious road down to Jericho (sub-tropical, "the city of Palm Trees"). Now, dazed by the merciless heat despite the later afternoon hour, our animals have to be urged to take the stony rise that leads to our destination ten kilometres (6 miles) south of Jericho. Let's give the donkeys a rest and look around. A kilometre to our left and some metres below us smoulders the dull Dead Sea with the mountains of Moab beyond. This strange sheet of water stretching 75 kilometres (50 miles) to the south is the lowest point on the earth's surface. To our right, stark cliffs rise to the formidable wilderness of Judea. The dark mouths of natural caves pock-mark the dismal eroded hillside. Subconscious dread of the place makes us dig our heels into the squat beasts; we ride and move on.

Then, towards the edge of the bluff ahead, quite incongruous, indeed almost laughable, rises a walled group of buildings and sounds of life. We have arrived.

We pass under the solidly-built tower which blocks out the sun and are courteously met and welcomed into a walled courtyard. Turning left through a narrow passage-way leads us to a wider court, where our donkeys are taken from us to the stables tucked away at the far end. We can see two men working rhythmically at the flat mill-stones grinding barley and from the bakery comes the enticing smell of newly-baked bread. A jug of surprisingly cool water is passed round to each of us and we drink gratefully. Our guide had ducked through a doorway to our left and is beckoning us to follow. The dark interior is bewildering but sweetly cool. Through an open doorway we glimpse silent men, studying leather and papyrus scrolls. But our guide wants to show us into the room ahead.

The room is tall, narrow and long. Down its length run stone tables and seated on stone benches men are studiously writing. The guide clears his throat.

The Qumran Community

"These two rooms are a focal point of the community buildings," he tells us. "In this room (the Scriptorium) the holy Law, the prophets and the sacred writings are most carefully copied as soon as a scroll shows signs of wear. Next door, in the library are hundreds of scrolls, not only of Scripture but also commentaries by our learned brethren on the prophets of old who foretold the coming of the hated Romans. Our brother, here, is copying the rule book of the community, *The Manual of Discipline*. If you young men wish to join us, you realise it will be two full years before you enter the Brotherhood at the discretion of the Council of Fifteen?"

"But why do you live in this hot and desert place?" one of us asks, sensing that none of us is yet ready to talk of becoming "volunteers for holiness" as they call it.

"We are the 'voice crying in the wilderness' that the prophet Isaiah speaks of, 'to prepare the way for the coming of the Lord' (Isaiah 40:3). We have separated ourselves from the tents of wickedness. We wait the coming of the two Messiahs of Priesthood and Kingship. We have waited a hundred years; we can wait another hundred. But at the End of days will come the War of the Children of Light against the Children of Darkness and then we shall know what to do; the plans are all here in the scrolls."

He goes on to tell us that although the scrolls are written in the new "square" Hebrew letters, when a scribe comes across *Yahweh*, the name of god, he cleans his pen, washes his hands and then uses the ancient Hebrew script for the Name. "When a worn scroll has been copied," he continues, "it is carefully wrapped in linen and placed in one of the caves in the hills . . . But I talk too long; it is time for you to take refreshment."

We now walk the full length of the big courtyard when, to the left, we witness an impressive sight. Through an open doorway we can see into a spacious hall some 20 metres long. Here about 70 men are gathered, eating in silence. One of their number has just mounted a raised platform at one end of the hall. He begins to read from a scroll, with dignity, to his attentive audience.

"The community is divided into three," our guide quietly informs us as he takes us to our tented accommodation outside the settlement. "Each group is on duty for eight hours, so that day and night, for the twenty-four hours of every day, the Scriptures are being read and copied and studied and so kept alive."

Disaster for Qumran

The Qumran Community we have just visited continued its quiet monastic existence "for another hundred years" as the guide had said. In 31 BC a violent earthquake formed giant cracks in some

Cave 4 (centre of picture) where most scrolls were found.

of the staircases and toppled out-buildings. They must have felt that "the End" had come. But they "picked up the pieces" and began the daily routine once more.

It was late in 66 AD (the Qumran community was active all through the life of Jesus) that signs of real trouble began. The Jewish people had been suffering the occupation of their country by the "hated Romans" now, for well over a century and revolution was in the air. By the year 68 AD the Romans were in control again everywhere except for the capital, Jerusalem, which it had under seige. One of the casualties (at the hands of the famous Tenth Legion) was the community at Qumran.

What happened exactly, we do not know. Presumably the whole settlement was wiped out by the Roman army. As the Romans advanced from Jericho, the community made an agonising decision—to spend precious days and hours hiding their library of scrolls. The place they chose was ideal. Inaccessible except for the most agile and yet within a couple of hundred metres of the settlement, they considerably enlarged a cave overlooking the dry riverbed of the wadi Qumran (now known as Cave 4). In it they hid over four hundred scrolls, of which over ninety were of Old Testament books(thirteen fairly complete copies of Deuteronomy, thirteen of Isaiah, ten of the Psalms and copies of every book of the Old Testament except the book of Esther). To make doubly sure, they carefully wrapped other scrolls and placed them in huge earthenware jugs, putting them in widely separated caves in the area. In one they placed their amazing copper scrolls which gave clues for the finding of the buried treasure of the community. (Un fortunately, no one knows exactly from where the clues start!)

All this feverish last-minute activity was in the hopes that one day they would be able to come back and start community life again, bringing their hidden library back into the quiet reading room at Qumran. But they never came back. Years passed, then centuries, nineteen centuries in fact.

The discovery of the Qumran scrolls

It was late February 1947 when a young Arab teenager, Muhammed-el-Dhib (''the wolf'') chanced on the discovery of a lifetime. Muhammed threw a stone into the mouth of one of the couple of hundred caves in the area, perhaps to chase a stray goat out or maybe for the sheer joy of throwing stones. His heart leapt within him as he heard the last sound he would have expected, the sound of breaking pottery. Coming back later with a friend, Muhammed found a number of jars, most of them broken when part of the roof had caved in, and within, foul-smelling bundles wrapped in linen, black with age.

Inside the linen bundles were rolls of leather with writing that they did not recognise.

Eventually, in fact over a year later, the seven scrolls Muhammed had chanced upon, reached the hands of experts and the story of the amazing Dead Sea Scrolls hit the headlines. It was of these first few scrolls that Professor Albright of the U.S.A. wrote that here was "the greatest manuscript discovery of modern times." Since then a careful search of surrounding caves has brought hundreds of scrolls and over 40,000 fragments back to the light of day.

Nor are even the tiniest fragments thrown away, although many are no bigger than your thumb. For some decades (since 1948), the most fascinating jig-saw puzzle of all time has been taking shape—the fitting together of these bits of leather back into their original scrolls.

Try an experiment: three of you write about a page on separate sheets of paper (you could copy different pages from this chapter for instance); now tear each page into roughly one-inch squares but don't tear neatly, and mingle the three sets of fragments. How will you be able to reassemble the pieces into the original sheets? Here are some clues:

(a) handwriting (no two people write exactly the same)
(b) the shape of one piece "marrying" to the next
(c) context (the logical order of words and sentences).

These are the basic principles experts are using with the damaged scrolls.

"But why bother?" you might ask, "Surely there are plenty of copies of these scrolls already."

Qumran and the Masoretic Text

The reason for all the excitement is best illustrated by the chart (below). But first a few simple but surprising facts. The oldest complete Old Testament written in Hebrew known to exist (before 1947) was a handwritten copy dating from 916 AD (strangely enough in a museum in Leningrad, Russia). About 700 AD a group of Jewish scholars living in Tiberias (a town on the west side of the Sea of Galilee) carefully studied all available manuscripts of the Old Testament (books written by hand—Latin *manus* = hand). They then decided upon what they considered the exact original wording of these books must have been. These scholars called themselves the "*Masoretes*" (Men of the Tradition) and so this text of the Old Testament is called the Masoretic Text. It is the basis of all translation of the Old Testament (from Hebrew) right up to 1947.

Can you see now why the Dead Sea Scrolls (more correctly called the Qumran Scrolls) are so important? Think it out. The oldest complete copy of the Hebrew Old Testament (before 1947) was the Masoretic Text of 916 AD; but the Qumran scrolls date from roughly 100 BC or earlier. Look at the chart.

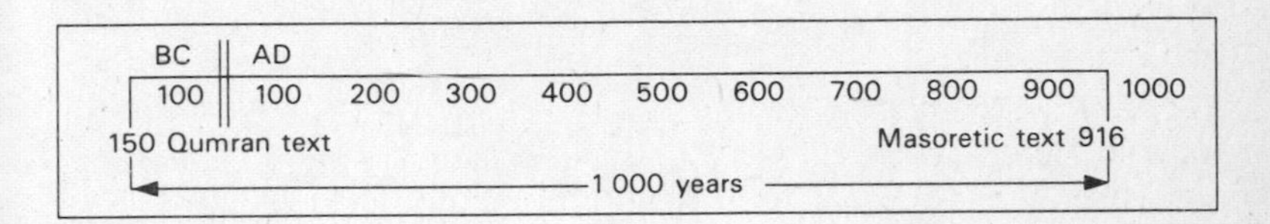

The Qumran scrolls are 1,000 years older than the document from which our Old Testament has been translated. A thousand years nearer to the original writings. Here is the Hebrew Old Testament text that Jesus must have known.

The question is: How accurate were the Masoretes in working out a reliable text? Or, to put it bluntly, how accurate is our Old Testament? The answer is astonishing. Let's see what an expert has to say: Professor Millar Burrows (Yale University) was in charge of the American School of Oriental Research in Jerusalem when the first scrolls were brought in.

> The six manuscripts of Genesis vary only at a few scattered points from the Masoretic Text . . . Isaiah was evidently the most popular of the prophetic books in the Qumran Community. In addition to the two scrolls from Cave 1 there are more or less extensive fragments of thirteen others from Cave 4. Like the incomplete scroll from Cave 1, the Cave 4 fragments agree closedly with the Masoretic Text.

How could the text remain so consistent over a thousand years? We shall look briefly into this question in the next chapter. But first we must spend a few minutes on another Old Testament collection that originated about 200 BC. Strangely enough it is in Greek. It is probably the earliest attempt to translate the Hebrew Bible.

The Greek Septuagint (LXX)

There is a rather fantastic legend that this translation of the Old Testament into Greek was completed in seventy-two days by seventy-two Jewish scholars in the city of Alexandria (North Egypt) about the year 258 BC. (Just to give you an idea of how long a translation actually takes, the New English Bible, which many of you use, took thirty men, thirteen years to complete!) However, what remains of the story is that the translation is now referred to as the Septuagint (Latin = seventy). The translation was probably made for the large Jewish community at Alexandria who spoke Greek not Hebrew. (It has been estimated that almost a million Jews were living in that area of Egypt in the second century BC). Fragments of the Old Testament books of Leviticus and Numbers in Greek were found in Cave 4 at Qumran.

LXX and the New Testament

But what makes the Septuagint (LXX) so interesting and important is that many New Testament writers, especially the Apostle Paul, quote from the LXX. The New Testament was, of course, written in Greek and was originally read by people who had little or no knowledge of the Hebrew language.

5. The Bible becomes a book

Koine Greek

The whole of the New Testament was written within a very few years (probably between about 40 and 90 AD) with the majority of it completed by 65 AD. The language of the New Testament is the Greek spoken throughout the Mediterranean lands by the ordinary people and, for that reason, called *Koine*(Greek for ''common'' and pronounced ''coin-ay''). Like all languages used over a wide area, Koine Greek varied considerably in different parts of the Mediterranean (in the same way, possibly, that there are marked differences between Australian, American and British English).

New Testament Greek

The Greek that Paul wrote in his letters, and that the Gospel writers used in their accounts of the life and teaching of Jesus, was strongly influenced by the Septuagint Old Testament. It was affected, too, by Aramaic which had become the everyday speech of the uneducated Jews (see page 5). Jesus, himself, could speak Aramaic as can be seen when he took the limp hand of a twelve year old girl who had just died, and said, "Talitha Cum" (Aramaic for "It's time to get up, young lady!"—Mark 5:41).

How books began

New Testament writers were continuously referring their readers back to the Old Testament. After all, the Old Testament was their Bible, since they themselves were writing to the New Testament. Take Paul's letter to the church at Rome (Epistle to the Romans). He quotes, in that single letter, from twenty-five different Old Testament books. Just suppose you were a believer living in Rome when the letter was received. What practical problem would face you if you wanted to look up all these quotations? (Well, we can tell you one problem that you probably won't have thought of. There would be no chapters and verses to tell you in what part of each scroll to look. So you would have to know all twenty-five books so well that you would know how far into each scroll to go to find the passage Paul was quoting.) But what physical difficulty would face you that you do not have with the neatly bound Bible you are now using?

You would have to take from your shelves (if you could afford them all) about twenty different scrolls of the Old Testament writings one at a time (some of the shorter books of the Bible were grouped into one scroll). It is because the early Christians were so Bible-centred in their preaching that the book form we are now familiar with became popular. In a sense, it is true to say that Christianity invented the book.

The Codex (or book)

The term used for the sewing together of folded pages written on both sides, is a *codex* (pl. *codices*). The whole Bible, instead of taking up forty or so bulky scrolls, could be confined to about three codices. The thickness of papyrus sheets still made it impossible to get the whole Bible into a single codex.

The next step, therefore, was to look around for a writing material thin enough to allow many more pages to be bound within one set of covers. That material, the earliest use of which is about 190 BC, was calf or antelope skin, known as vellum (''veal'' is your butcher's name for calf's meat). In fact it is so thin that usually it was doubled (with the original rough hair side facing inwards). Of the two earliest fairly complete Bibles yet discovered (Old Testament Septuagint (Greek) and New Testament combined) one, Codex Sinaiticus, had well over three hundred and fifty pages each roughly thirty-five centimetres square with four columns of writing per page; and the second, the Vatican manuscript, has seven hundred and fifty-nine pages, measuring twenty-six centimetres square with three columns on each page. The exciting discovery of the first of these in a waste-paper basket, in 1844, is well worth reading and we shall later on give you extracts from the finder's personal diary and tell how the manuscript was eventually sold to the British Museum for £100,000.

Copying the text

Now that we have met, for the first time, a couple of complete Bibles in book form (the two codices just referred to date from about 350 AD) we must discuss how these documents were copied. Firstly, it is essential to understand that, for the first three thousand years (from the earliest original Biblical writings of, say, about 1450 BC up to the invention of printing in the 1450's AD) every copy of the Bible or any part of it, had to be written laboriously by hand. A complete Bible took one man about ten months to write. Immediately you can see how expensive a complete Bible would be.

1. the cost of materials—e.g. enough animals killed to provide the parchment or vellum; or, the importing of high quality papyrus in sufficient quantities. (The papyrus would all have to be hand-made, of course).
2. virtually a year's salary for the scribe whom you paid to make the copy—and, remember, he would be a well-educated man and would charge accordingly.

ΕΝΑΡΧΗΗΝΟ̄ΛΟΓΟΣΚΑΙΟΛΟΓΟΣΗ̄
ΠΡΟΣΤΟΝΘ̄Ν̄·ΚΑΙΘ̄Σ̄ΗΝΟΛΟΓΟΣ·
ΟΥΤΟΣΗΝΕΝΑΡΧΗΠΡΟΣΤΟΝΘ̄Ν̄
ΠΑΝΤΑΔΙΑΥΤΟΥΕΓΕΝΕΤΟ·ΚΑΙΧΩ
ΡΕΙΣΑΥΤΟΥΕΓΕΝΕΤΟΟΥΔΕΕΝ·
ΟΓΕΓΟΝΕΝΕΝΑΥΤΩΖΩΗΗΝ·
ΚΑΙΗΖΩΗΗΝΤΟΦΩΣΤΩΝΑΝΩ̄Ν̄
ΚΑΙΤΟΦΩΣΕΝΤΗΣΚΟΤΙΑΦΑΙ
ΝΕΙ·ΚΑΙΗΣΚΟΤΙΑΑΥΤΟΟΥΚΑΤΕ
ΛΑΒΕΝ· ΕΓΕΝΕΤΟΑΝΟ̄Σ̄ΑΠΕ
ΣΤΑΛΜΕΝΟΣΠΑΡΑΘ̄ῩΟΝΟΜΑΑΥ
ΤΩΪΩΑΝΝΗΣ·ΟΥΤΟΣΗΛΘΕΝ
ΕΙΣΜΑΡΤΥΡΙΑΝΪΝΑΜΑΡΤΥΡΗ
ΣΗΠΕΡΙΤΟΥΦΩΤΟΣ·ΪΝΑΠΑΝ
ΤΕΣΠΙΣΤΕΥΣΩΣΙΝΔΙΑΥΤΟΥ·

INTHEBEGINNINGWASTHEWORDANDTHEWORDWAS
WITHGD·ANDGDWASTHEWORD·
HEWASINTHEBEGINNINGWITHGD
ALLWEREMADEBYHIMANDWITH
OUTHIMWASMADENOTONE*THING*
THATWASMADEINHIMLIFEWAS
ANDTHELIFEWASTHELIGHTOFMN
ANDTHELIGHTINDARKNESSSHIN
ETHANDTHEDARKNESSDIDNOTITCOMPRE
HEND· THEREWASAMNSE

NTFROMGODWHOSENAME*WAS*
IOHN·THIS*PERSON*CAME
ASAWITNESSTHATHEMIGHTTESTI
FYCONCERNINGTHELIGHTTHATA
LLMIGHTBELIEVETHROUGHHIM·

Codex Alexandrinus

No wonder very few people could afford their own personal copies of the Bible in earlier times. There is evidence that the early Christian communities (*ekklesias* as they were called = ''the called-out people'' met regularly to hear readings from scrolls and codices of the Bible, owned by wealthy members and that this formed the basis of their children's education.

Certain devices were used to save space. Hebrew had no vowels (although small dots and strokes under or over letters to represent vowel sounds, called ''pointing'', began to be introduced as early as the Qumran scroll of Isaiah found in Cave 1). Both Hebrew and Greek were written without any distinction between capital and small letters. One way of assessing the age of a Greek manuscript is by the style of writing. The Codex Sinaiticus and the Vatican manuscript are both in uncials (capital letters) which immediately tells us that they must have been written before about 850 AD when this style was replaced entirely by a running (cursive) style, similar to our own ''joined'' writing.

What will surprise you is that, to further save space, they left no gaps between words, and abbreviations of Greek words were frequently made. Only a minimum of punctuation was used (it is because of the lack of punctuation that we can date these two manuscripts before 550 AD). The illustration from the Codex Alexandrinus (approximately 520 AD) gives the actual Greek on the left and as close an English equivalent as can be made, on the right. Note the abbreviations and the words running into one another.

This Codex Alexandrinus is an interesting manuscript, in four volumes, with an intriguing note scribbled in Arabic claiming that it was written by ''Thecla, the Martyr''. (This cannot be true since at least four styles of handwriting are evident, and anyway Thecla lived in Alexandria at about 390 AD and these codices are not that old). What is significant is that *Thecla was a lady* and that we can therefore assume that women might have been copyists of Bible manuscripts as well as men.

Rules for Scribes

The rules which applied to those who copied Biblical writings were very strict, especially for the Hebrew documents. Here are some which applied to the copying of the Masoretic text:

1. each line must consist of thirty letters
2. each column must have an even number of lines, and that same number throughout the scroll
3. the whole scroll must be carefully ruled up with lines before a word is written
4. the ink must be black, made from soot, charcoal and honey mixed into a paste and then allowed to harden. (This cake of ink, like paint in a paint box, was then moistened by a special solution of water and gums)
5. no letter or word shall be written from memory
6. each word must be studied in the original and then spoken aloud before being copied
7. the book of Deuteronomy must end on the last line of a column . . . and so on. Word, and even letter counts were made and the whole scroll then checked by a supervisor.

Greek scribes were not quite so hedged in by regulations for the copying of manuscripts. Sometimes a method of dictation was used so that many copies could be made at the same time (one man reading from the original, whilst several others wrote down what he said).

This, then, is the Bible's story, in its original languages of Hebrew and Greek, and how the text was preserved as the result of careful copying. In the next section we are going to look at some of the men who undertook the translation of the Bible into the English version you have in front of you.

PART TWO

The English Bible

1. When it began

The first complete Bible in English was not translated from Hebrew or Greek, but from Latin. You may already have wondered why, in the first century Roman Empire, Koine Greek should have been more widely spoken than Latin. The fact is that the Roman Empire, as such, was little more than 50 years old when Jesus was born and was destined to control its vast dominions for another 500 years. The situation in Judea at the time of Christ's crucifixion is illustrated by the inscription on the cross. "This is Jesus of Nazareth, the King of the Jews" (John 19:19). This notice was written in Hebrew (the official religious and legal language of the Jews); in Greek (the language spoken by educated and business people); in Latin (the language of the Roman authorities such as Pontius Pilate).

The Latin Vulgate—404 AD

By about 170 AD Latin was replacing Greek as the common language of the Empire, especially in North Africa. It is not surprising therefore, that parts of the Bible began to be translated into Latin. This work was done in a rather haphazard, rough-and-ready way. Christianity became the official religion of the Empire early in the fourth century. In 382 AD Pope Damasus commissioned his secretary (Jerome) to make a revision of all these Old Latin versions, checking them against the Greek. Jerome went to live and work in Bethlehem and there completed, over a period of twenty years, what was really a fresh translation of the whole Bible into Latin. He learnt Hebrew, so that he could translate the Old Testament; not only from the Greek Septuagint, but also from its original language. The Latin he used was that spoken by the common people, so that, just as the New Testament had originally been written in Koine (Common) Greek, now the first official Latin version came to be called the Latin Vulgate (Latin *vulgaris* ® common). This Latin Vulgate, completed in 404 AD, gradually became the recognised Bible of the Roman Catholic church, even after the fall of the Roman Empire.

It was the Vulgate, therefore, that reached the British Isles with the first Christian preachers. It was the Vulgate that the monks so painstakingly copied by hand, adding the illuminated initial letters and pictures which made Bible manuscripts a work of art. And it was from the Latin Vulgate that the first attempt at a complete Bible in English was made in 1382.

Wycliffe and the first Bible in English

John Wycliffe was born in the North of England in 1324 and soon proved a very clever student. He went to Oxford where he lectured in theology and became Master of the famous Balliol College when only about forty. He inspired his university students to spend their vacations preaching to villagers and farm labourers. It soon became necessary to quote from the Bible in English, and as a result he began his translation with the help of two colleagues, Nicholas Hereford and John Purvey.

The first attempt (1382) was very stilted and did not read like English; but the final edition (1395, ten years after Wycliffe's death and largely the work of John Purvey), was a great improvement. Here is Luke's story of the angel's message to the shepherds at the birth of Jesus:

> Soothly (truly) I evangelize (preach) to you great joy that shall be to all people. For a saviour is born today to us, that is Christ, a Lord, in the city of David. And this shall be a token to you. You shall find the child wrapped in clothes and put in a creche . . . Glory in the highest things of God and in earth peace to men of good will.
> (Luke 2:10–12)

The church did not approve of Wycliffe's translation largely because he used it to determine its authority, contrasting as he did, "Bible Law" and "Church Law". Many of the first translators of the Bible into English were persecuted, some were killed, not so much for translating the Bible as for the teachings they said it contained. After Wycliffe's death a new Law was introduced (1408):

> that no one henceforth on his own authority translate any text of Holy Scripture into English or other language . . . and that no book of this kind be read, either already composed in the time of the said John Wycliffe, or since then, or that may in future be composed . . . until the translation itself shall have been approved . . .

The reference here to "reading" as well as translating, is important. Wycliffe's followers (known as Lollards—"mutterers", by his enemies) read from the translation in market places and open fields. Many ordinary people, who could not themselves read, listened attentively and could recite whole passages and even complete Books of the Bible from memory (and were imprisoned for doing so). In 1428, as an example to others who might attempt unauthorised translations, Wycliffe's body was taken out of the grave, where it had lain for forty years, and his bones burned. The ashes were then thrown into the River Swift (at Lutterworth where he had been priest) and so, as one of his followers put it, "his teaching spread into the ocean and is now dispersed over all the world." One of the societies for the translation of the Bible into modern languages is called the Wycliffe Bible Society in memory of this courageous pioneer.

2. The Incredible 1450's

What would have happened to the development of the English Bible had it not been for a German with the improbable name of Johann Gensfleisch (Gooseflesh!) it is impossible to say. Even Johann was not too happy with his surname, so he changed it to his mother's maiden name and called himself Johann Gutenberg.

Printing—1454

It is wrong to credit Gutenberg with the invention of printing. When the children of Israel were still in Egypt, (1500 BC) the neighbouring, powerful Empire of the Hittites was actually printing letters by impressing individual stamps onto clay. The Chinese, too, had been printing fabrics for centuries.

What Gutenberg introduced was the use of movable type by which complete pages of individual metal letters could be made up into words and sentences and printed at one time. This forme (frame containing the type) could print four to eight pages at once (depending on the page size). It would take one day to set the type and then about 1500 copies were printed, one at a time. The type was then distributed and the next forme made up. The first book Gutenberg printed was the Latin Vulgate Bible in 1454. It had 1 282 pages and took about two years to set and print. The first printed Bible was done on parchment which Gutenberg's mother had prepared for the work.

The importance of printing is impossible to overestimate. As we have seen, a handwritten Bible would take ten months to write and cost an educated man's annual salary to buy. And now, as a Bishop said of a printer a few years after Gutenberg, "He prints as much in a day as was formerly written in a year."

Perhaps this is a good opportunity to remember that even these first printed Bibles did not have the chapters and verses we know today. Gutenberg put a letter of the alphabet (A,B,C, etc) in the margin, every fifteen lines or so for each book of the Bible for ease of reference. He deliberately used the heavy black letter type-face to make his printed page look as much like a written one as possible, even adding illuminiated initial letters, as in a manuscript.

The Renaissance and old manuscripts

Whilst Gutenberg was making his break-through in printing, other equally momentous events were in motion. In May 1453 a frightening yet vastly important incident took place. The Moslem Empire of Turkey spread across the narrow straits which divide Asia and Europe. The Christian city of Constantinople was engulfed, the Turks actually reaching the gates of Vienna before they were halted. Even now, five hundred years later, the ancient city of Constantinople (now Istanbul) still belongs to Turkey.

Not unlike the Qumran Community, the scholars and priests of Constantinople took care to carry their priceless Greek manuscripts with them as they fled into exile to Italy and France. Pope Nicholas V bought from them 5,000 of these manuscripts, which became the basis of the Vatican Library in Rome. Amongst these treasures of the past was the Codex Vaticanus, already mentioned (page 26) which remains the oldest and most complete bible in Greek yet discovered.

We call the years that followed, the Renaissance (re-birth), because of the rediscovery not only of early manuscripts of the bible, but also of plays, poems and books of science Greek writers of pre-Christian times. This great revival of interest in learning and culture brought with it a renewed enthusiasm for the Greek language. The hundred or so newly-discovered early copies of the New Testament and of the Septuagint began to be compared during the next forty years. (The Old Testament in Hebrew was, of course, always available at Jewish Synogogues.)

The manuscripts and the Reformation

A comparison between the Greek texts, suddenly made available, and Jerome's Latin Vulgate, revealed that certain of the church's teachings appeared to be based on Jerome's translation of words and phrases which the Greek did not seem to support.

Not that the Church's detractors could agree. The only thing that united them was the need to bring about reform in the Church. And so we call this new development, the Reformation.

The Reformation is the third great development of the fifteenth century to have lasting effect on the story of the English Bible, as we shall see.

This short chapter has contained such important matters that we must summarise them for easy reference:

1. May 1453—the Turks take Constantinople and Christian scholars flee to the west with precious Greek manuscripts (many of Biblical books).

2. November 1454—first printed Bible (latin Vulgate)—Gutenberg.
3. The Reformation arose, in part, when scholars began to compare the newly-found manuscripts with the Latin Vulgate. Textual variations were used as evidence for the need to reform practices and doctrines in the church.

3. The Greatest Translator of them all

If you like reading about smuggling and midnight flits, about spies and strangling, this is the story for you.

William Tyndale, like John Wycliffe before him, was a highly intelligent man. By his twenty-first birthday he had a Master's degree from Oxford and was an ordained priest. He is said to have spoken seven languages fluently. He made the first translations into English direct from Hebrew and Greek and these brilliant translations have been the basis of almost all English versions for the past 400 years, until this century.

Erasmus and the Greek Text

Two men had an important influence on Tyndale's work. The first was Erasmus, whose edited Greek text Tyndale used. Erasmus was born in Rotterdam in 1466 and became one of Europe's leading authorities on the ancient Greek language. Although Erasmus refused to join in the Reformation, his work on editing the Greek text of the New Testament by comparing manuscripts discovered during the Renaissance showed that the Vulgate was not always accurate and in fact Erasmus himself published his own Latin version alongside the Greek and Latin text, Erasmus had this to say:

> Would that these were translated into each and every language so that they might be read and understood not only by Scots and Irishmen, but also by Turks [remember that the Turks were invading eastern Europe as Erasmus wrote] . . . Would that the farmer might sing snatches of the Scriptures at his plough and that the weaver might hum phrases of Scripture to the tune of his shuttle.

Martin Luther and the German Bible

Martin Luther was the first to make a translation using the Greek text edited by Erasmus. This lively little man, Luther, has been called the Father of the Reformation and even today there are still Lutheran churches which base much of their teaching on his translations and commentaries.

Although he had been a monk for seven years, in 1512 he began to have doubts (just as Wycliffe had before him) about the teaching and practices of the Church. After five years of study and attempts to reform the Church from within he felt so convinced of his new thinking that, at the risk of death and the certainty of being thrust out of the Church, he made his ideas public by literally nailing them to the church door in Wittenberg. In 1521 his case was considered and he was condemned to death, in his absence.

Luther escaped to the village of Wartburg and there immediately began his translation of the New Testament, into German. Luther believed that the only way for the Scriptures to be ''read by the farmer'' was to mix with these people and listen carefully to the way they spoke. Partly because he was a wanted man and also in order to meet the common people, Luther disguised himself and spent almost a year alternating between his translating and chatting to the peasants about everyday things so that his German New Testament would be lively and up-to-date. By September 1522 the book was printed and was spreading rapidly throughout Europe. His translation of the Old Testament took much longer, (it is three times as long as the New Testament) the whole Bible not being ready until 1532.

William Tyndale and the English Bible

One man to get an early copy of Luther's German New Testament was William Tyndale. Since we last saw him, taking his MA at Oxford, he had spent a year at Cambridge University polishing up his Greek and in particular studying Erasmus's Greek text of the New Testament. He read what Erasmus had written in his Preface and now Tyndale decided:

> If God spare my life, e're many years, I will cause a boy that drives the plough to know more Scripture than the priests.

Early Bible Translations & Printing

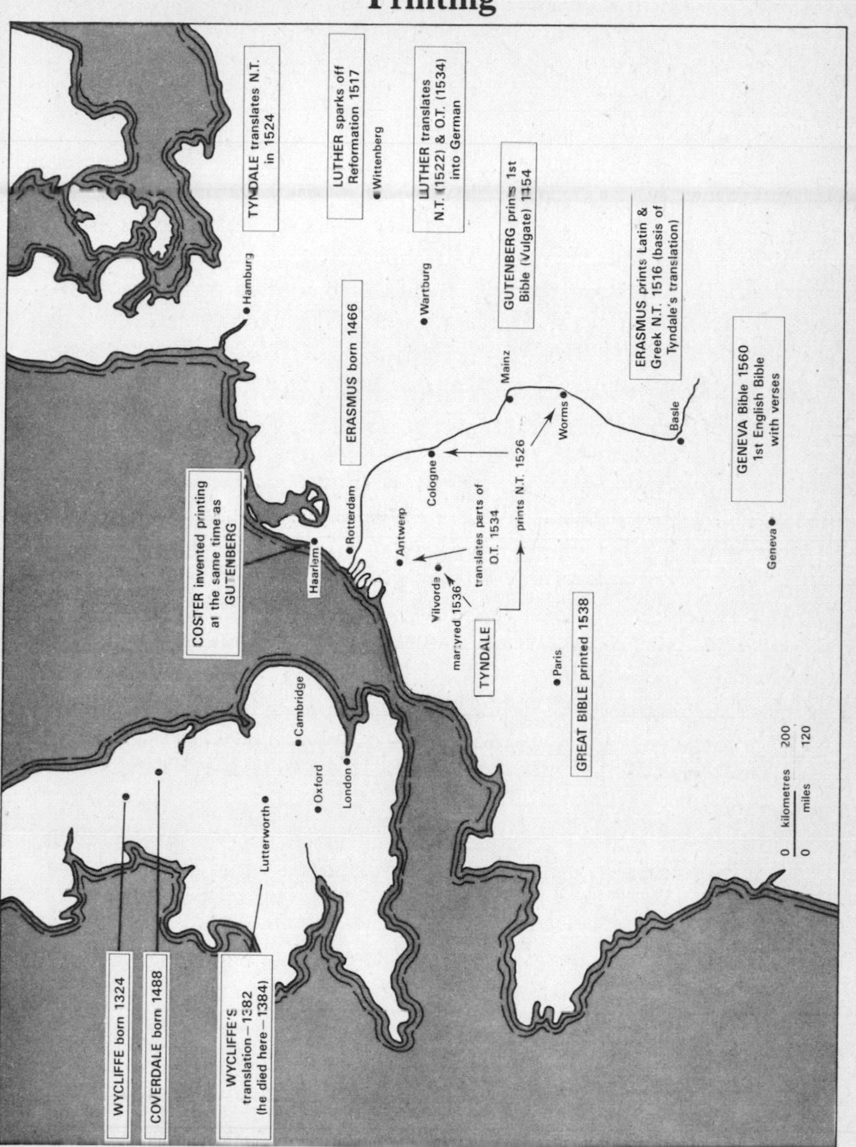

He tried to interest influential people in his translation, even applying to the Bishop of London, but with no success and finally he gave up trying in 1524:

> I understood, at last, not only that there was no room in my Lord of London's palace to translate the New Testament, but also that there was no place to do it in all England.

For the rest of his life, which was to be only twelve years, he lived in exile and in almost daily fear of imprisonment and violent death. He was just over forty when they caught him and executed him.

Tyndale's New Testament—1525

Tyndale went first to Hamburg, which was sympathetic to the Reformation, and there he worked rapidly, producing his first translation of the New Testament early in 1525. He used the Vulgate, Erasmus's Greek and Latin Testament and Luther's German version. Now to get it printed. Tyndale decided on Cologne since it would be possible to ship the books down the River Rhine to the North Sea, and thence to carefully selected ports on the east coast of England. The whole smuggling network had been worked out before Tyndale left England. A group of London businessmen, calling themselves the Society of Christian Brethren, financed and planned the whole operation. They knew the distribution system would work—its European connection was already being used for Luther's New Testament.

Spies of the Bishop of London, who had refused Tyndale permission to make his English translation, nearly ruined the project. Warned in the nick of time, Tyndale slipped away up river to Worms and there the printing was completed. Thus 100,000 copies of Tyndale's New Testament were smuggled into England.

It has been computed that a farm labourer would have needed to save all his earnings for thirteen years to be able to buy one manuscript (handwritten) copy of Wycliffe's Bible. A copy of Tyndale's (printed) New Testament cost him one week's wages. No wonder it has been said "Printing invented the Reformation."

Further Translations by Tyndale

Tyndale now set to work on the Old Testament, studying Hebrew with great enthusiasm and success. He moved to Antwerp in Belgium where he was safe for the first time after leaving England, since Antwerp was a "free", independent city. In 1534 he had translated the first five Books (Genesis to Deuteronomy), the Book of Jonah and some of the Old Testament historical Books. A complete revision of his New Testament was also published that year. Then the blow fell. Tricked into leaving Antwerp, Tyndale was imprisoned at Vilvorde Castle (not far from Brussels). A letter written from prison reads:

> Be kind enough to send a warmer cap, for I suffer extremely from perpetual catarrh, which is much increased by this cell . . . a warmer coat also, for that which I have is very thin; also a piece of cloth to patch my leggings—my shirts are worn out too . . .

But the letter ends, so characteristically,

> Also persuade the keeper that he would suffer me to have my Hebrew Bible and grammar and dictionary.

Tyndale's contribution to Bible translation is difficult to appreciate, but here are a couple of points for you to consider. After the English Bible had been thoroughly revised in 1885, 81 per cent of the New Testament was still in Tyndale's wording of 1534. Secondly, when Tyndale could not find a word which exactly expressed in English the Greek or Hebrew idea, he made up an English word. When you see what some of these new words were, you will realise the impact this man has made on our language:
"broken-hearted"; "scapegoat"; "godly"; "godliness"; and "ungodly"; "peacemaker"; and (would you believe it) "beautiful".

Tyndale's Death—1536

On Friday 6th October, 1536, Tyndale was strangled at the stake outside Vilvorde Castle and then burnt to ashes (as Wycliffe's body had been a hundred years before). His last words were, "Lord, open the King of England's eyes." This dying man's prayer was already being answered, as we shall see in the next section.

4. The Age of Translations

No century, until our own, has produced so many translations of the Bible as the sixteenth. There were nine important versions in English between Tyndale's work (1534) and the Authorised Version (King James) of 1611. We shall not look at all of them but so that you can place those we mention, here is a useful date chart.

Year	Translation	Ruler of England
1534	Tynedale (NT and parts of OT from original languages	Henry VIII (founded Church of England 1534)
1535	Coverdale (1st complete Bible from original languages)	
1537	Matthew's	
1539	Taverner's	
1539	Great (1st "Appointed to be read in churches")	
		Edward VI
		Mary (Rom. Catholic)
1560	Geneva ("Reformation" translation)	
1564	Shakespeare born	Elizabeth I
1568	Bishops (C of E 'reply' to Geneva)	
1582	Rheims NT (Rom. Catholic trans.)	
1609	Douai (whole Bible–Rom. Catholic)	James I (U.K.)
1611	Authorised (King James) Version	

Coverdale—first printed Bible in English—1535

Like Martin Luther, the Englishman Miles Coverdale had been an Augustinian monk, before becoming involved (in 1528) in the Reformation. Forced to leave England, there is evidence that he joined Tyndale in Hamburg in 1529 and helped that great translator with his Old Testament work. Coverdale admitted that he was "no scholar in Hebrew or Greek," but he had the same sensitivity for language as Luther and Tyndale had.

Coverdale (who was six years older than Tyndale) completed his translation of the whole bible in 1535 (the year Tyndale was captured and imprisoned at Vilvorde).

The second edition of Coverdale's Bible (1537) was the first Bible to be printed in England and bears the amazing words on the title page, "Set forth with the King's most gracious licence." What an astounding answer to Tyndale's prayer of the previous October, "Lord, open the King of England's eyes!"

Henry VIII and the Church of England—1534

What happened was that King Henry VIII of England had quarrelled with the Roman Catholic church so violently because it refused to allow him to divorce his wife, that he had decided to establish the Church in England under his authority, separate from Rome. Thus, in 1538, a year after, the Church of England came into existence. And the English church needed an English Bible. Coverdale's first version was chosen.

The great Bible—1539

Two years after the second edition thus licensed by King Henry, Coverdale was commissioned to edit a new version, based on translations from the original languages, which would become the new Church's official Bible, "appointed to be read in all churches."

This new Coverdale version is called the Great Bible (published April 1539) because it was deliberately made with large type and pages (for 40 cms × 28 cms) so that it could be easily read from in church. Every parish church was required by law to have a copy, with a fine for every month beyond the deadline (November 1,

1541) if they did not possess a copy. The first edition was printed in Paris because of the high quality of the de Colines Press, there. Coverdale went to Paris to see the book through to the final print (see also Preface).

Geneva Bible—1560

With the succession of Henry's daughter, Queen Mary, came bitter persecution of the new Church of England, since Mary was a Roman Catholic.

Once more Coverdale crossed the English Channel, this time making his way to Geneva in Switzerland. Geneva had become one of the key cities of the Reformation. There, two of its greatest leaders, Calvin and Knox, lived and a large number of exiled Englishmen made it their home until the end of Queen Mary's reign. The idea of yet another, fresh translation was discussed. William Whittingham (Calvins's brother-in-law) was already working on a fresh English New Testament, to contain notes, and, for ease of cross-reference between the various books, the first use of verse divisions.

Chapters and verses

The division of the Bible into the chapters we use today, was invented by Archbishop Stephen Langton (d 1228). Wycliffe's translation included these chapters. Verses were first included in Robert Stephens' Greek New Testament text (1551) printed by his father-in-law, de Colines of Paris, who had printed the Great Bible. Stephens is said to have completed the division of the New Testament during a long coach journey across France. The Old Testament had been divided into verses by Rabbi Nathan (1448). The Geneva Bible we are now to discuss (1560) is the first English bible to use these chapters and verses.

The Geneva Bible and Study Aids

The text of the Geneva Bible was undoubtedly the most accurate of all the English Bibles to that date (1560). But it is a Bible with an amazing number of quite new ideas. It is the first Bible to use our Roman type face (not the black letter that Gutenberg had invented). It has very full margins to help the reader understand the text, and many maps and illustrations. As we have just seen it is also the first English Bible to have both chapters and verses and as a result to have cross-references between books of the Bible in the margin. It also used italic printing where an English word is added to make sense but has no exact equivalent in the original Hebrew or Greek. The Geneva Bible was usually printed with a list of names in the Bible and their meanings and a simple index to "principal matters" in the Bible. Such a useful Bible obviously became popular. The first edition was out in time to be dedicated to the new Queen of England, Elizabeth 1 (another daughter of Henry VIII, who became like her father the head of the Church of England). The Geneva Bible is the one Shakespeare quotes from in his plays. This Bible went through 140 editions (each of several thousand) until it was no longer printed after 1644. Copies were still being used as family Bibles in England last century.

5. The Bible that moulded our language

Way back in the year 378 AD, a courageous man set off north from Greece into the barbarous interior of central Europe. His mission, to convert the Goths; his name, Bishop Ulfilas. Ulfilas, like many before and since, found that Christianity is a religion that needs a Book—the Bible—for its growth. His main problem was that the Goths had no books, in fact, so far as we know, no writing at all.

Ulfilas had to listen most carefully to the speech-sounds of the Goths and try to set them down using, basically, our Roman alphabet. Then he had to puzzle out how the language worked—its grammar. And, at last, to write the Bible down in the language he had reconstructed. The Bible was the beginning of reading and writing for the Goths. A most beautiful example of Ulfilas's Gothic translation of the Gospels can be seen at Uppsala University in Sweden. It has silver letters on violet-dyed vellum.

Examples of a similar kind are happening around us even today. Several African languages, for example, never had a written form until it was necessary that converts to Christianity had their

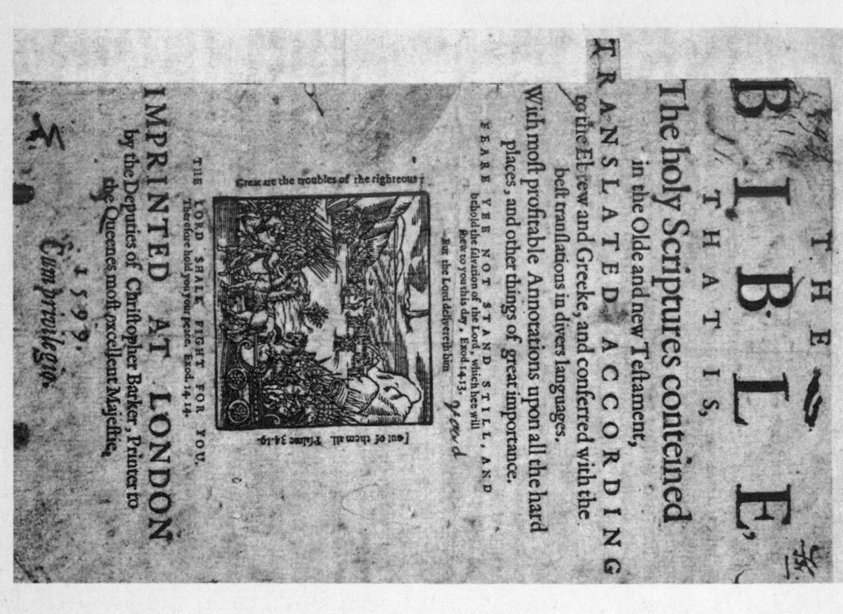

Thomas Wales took Ship on ye
19th Day of May, 1780 &
Sailed from Wainfleet Haven
ye 20 in ye Evening, with Captain
Douns on board a Collier; O
my Son my Son;

May Heaven's Choisist blessings
Wait on the
May thou be blest by Land & Sea
but O a tender Mother's Love
nether time nor Distance Can remove
Kind Heaven hear & pitty me,
Restore my Son in Safaty

Lucey Jonson Departed this
Life March the 1798, aged
2 years,

THE
BIBLE,
THAT IS,
The holy Scriptures conteined
in the Olde and new Testament,
TRANSLATED ACCORDING
to the Ebrew and Greeke, and conferred with the
best translations in divers languages.
With most profitable Annotations upon all the hard
places, and other things of great importance.

FEARE YEE NOT, STAND STILL, AND
behold the saluation of the Lord, which hee will
shew to you this day. Exod. 14. 13.

Great are the troubles of the righteous: But the Lord deliuereth him out of them all. Psalme 34. 19.

THE LORD SHALL FIGHT FOR YOU.
Therefore hold you your peace. Exod. 14. 14.

IMPRINTED AT LONDON
by the Deputies of Christopher Barker, Printer to
the Queenes most excellent Maiestie.
1599.
Cum privilegio.

Geneva Bible

own Bibles, and literacy began for them. This is why books and newspapers in African languages, for instance, use our alphabet.

The Authorised (King James) Version—1611

The case with the English language is not so dramatic, but no less real. Without the Authorised (or King James) Version of the Bible, English would be a different language. This version of the Bible, far more than Shakespeare, who had written all his plays by the date of its publication (1611), shaped the English language for the next three hundred years.

The first reason for this is that the Bible is a book that makes you think and, in the end, can actually change a man's thinking. Secondly, this particular version became the Bible used in almost every English church and chapel until the 1950's.

When the only book people read aloud was the Authorised Version of the Bible—and this was the case for centuries—then its words and phrases became part of the everyday speech of the English people, for example, "by the skin of my teeth" (Job 19:20); "in the twinkling of an eye" (I Cor. 15:52); "can a leopard change his spots?" (Jer. 13:23).

When King James, Elizabeth's nephew, came to the throne in 1603 he became the first King of the United Kingdom. He was already King of Scotland when his aunt died, and as her nearest relative, he agreed to unite England and Scotland as a new Kingdom. Early in his reign, he decided that there were too many translations of the Bible in English (see chart page 38) and that a new translation, which he would authorise, was necessary.

The King James (Authorised) Version was a revision of all previous translations into English, therefore, specially ordered by the king himself. The Bible was divided into five parts, each section having its own committee of translators. They had not only all of the English translations we have mentioned but also Hebrew, Greek and Latin texts as well. Time and time again, they found out how well Tyndale and Coverdale had done their work, although over eighty years had passed since the first edition of Tyndale's New Testament.

We leave this magnificent Bible with the opening words of the Translators' Preface. It is a sentence which deserves discussion:

Translation it is that openeth the window, to let in the light.

Printers' Errors

Printing Bibles is a very serious matter and almost as much care is taken over it as the old Masoretes took over the Hebrew scrolls. But mistakes are sometimes made. In the very first edition of the AV in 1611 by Robert Barker of London, for some odd reason Exodus 14:10 is repeated, word for word. So if you have a Bible with two verse 10's in this chapter of Exodus hang on to it!

Then there was the unfortunate edition of 1641 in which the printer left out the word *not* from Exodus 20:14 (look it up and you will realise why the printer was fined £300).

Finally, there must have been some red ears in the type setting room in 1702 when the first complaint came in about Psalm 119:161. It read, "Printers (it should read "Princes") have persecuted me without a cause." (No reference to the printers of this book, of course.)

6. Ancient Manuscripts and Modern Versions

Codex Sinaiticus Again

> It was at the foot of Mount Sinai, in the Convent of St. Catherine, that I discovered the pearl of all my researches in April, 1844. In visiting the library of the monastery, I perceived in the middle of the great hall, a large basket full of old parchments. What was my surprise to find amid this heap of papers a considerable number of sheets of a copy of the Old Testament in Greek, which seemed to me to be one of the most ancient that I had ever seen. I was allowed to possess myself of a third of these parchments (about forty-three sheets) all the more readily as they were destined for the fire. But I could not get them to yield up the remainder. The too lively satisfaction which I had displayed had aroused their suspicions as to the value of the manuscripts.

Thus the priceless Codex Sinaiticus was saved from being thrown into the heating furnace at St. Catherine's Monastery. So far, however, Count Tischendorf, who tells his own story, had only forty-three sheets. Years of intrigue followed until at last, backed by the Emperor of Russia, Tischendorf returned to St. Catherine's in January 1859. He was courteously received, but could find no further pages of the Codex that he knew must be there. On the last evening of his stay he was taking a walk in the walled garden, when a monk invited him into his cell for refreshments. They had been chatting about Greek copies of

The Monastery of St. Catherine (Sinai)

the Old Testament when the monk got up, casually enough, and said,

> 'And I, too, have read a Septuagint,'' and so saying, he took down from the corner of the room a bulky kind of volume, wrapped up in red cloth, and laid it before me. I unrolled the cover, and discovered, to my great surprise, not only those very fragments which, fifteen years before, I had taken out of the basket, but also other parts of the Old Testament and the New Testament complete. Full of joy, which this time I had the self-command to conceal, I asked, as if in a careless way, for permission to take the manuscript to my room to look over it more at leisure. There by myself I could give way to the transport of joy which I felt. I knew that I held in my hand the most precious Biblical treasure in existence . . .

But it was not until November 1859 that he was finally able to deliver it to St. Petersburg (now Leningrad) in Russia since the money had been donated by the Tsar of Russia. After the Russian Revolution of 1917, which brought the communists into power, discussions began in the UK to try to purchase the manuscript. Eventually in 1933 the British Museum had to pay the astonishing figure of £100,000, still the highest figure ever paid for a book. Almost all the money was donated by the general public.

Revised Version—1885

Because of this marvellous find and the discovery of many more manuscripts much older than had been available to the Authorised (King James) Version translators, it was decided that a revision of this famous version should be made.

Apart from inaccuracies of the text in small details, the actual English of the Authorised Version (AV) was becoming out of date. One simple example is the use of the word *let*. Today this means to *allow*, but it used to mean the exact opposite, as in Romans 1:13. In the AV, it tells how Paul had often wanted to go to Rome, but had been *let* (prevented) hitherto.

The Revised Version was completed in 1885. Seventy of the leading scholars of the Nineteenth century, from all major churches (including Roman Catholic) together with the great Hebrew authority, Ginsberg, (a Jew), were involved in the work.

American Standard—1901

An American team (which included Lutheran and Dutch Reformed Ministers) produced their revision in 1901.

With the discovery in the 1920's of hundreds more ancient manuscripts, came another flood of translations outpacing those exciting years in the 1500's when Erasmus had started modern scholarship on its momentous journey towards an ever more accurate text of the Bible.

The Revised Standard Version—1952

The first version to avail itself of the texts of the Dea Sea Scrolls (see page 21) was the American Revised Standard Version (RSV) one of the most reliable translations to work from, although somewhat hampered by its own rules as a revision (of the 1901 version) rather than a fresh translation. A slightly edited version of the RSV has now been approved for use by Roman Catholics and is called the 'Common Bible' (1973).

Jerusalem Bible (1966) and earlier Catholic Translations

The very first Roman Catholic translation of the Bible into English had been completed just over a year before the AV (late in 1609). The translation had to be made outside England, since it was then the Catholics who were persecuted (Elizabeth I was Queen). The University of Douai (in northern France) had an English college attached to it for Catholic exiles. This Douai Version (as it is called) was far too full of Latin-based words to be successful. It was translated from the Latin Vulgate (see page 30), as was the much more recent Catholic version by Ronald Knox (1949) although in both these cases the original languages were consulted.

Other important "committee" translations followed the RSV. The first of these was published in 1966 and has an interesting history. It is called the Jerusalem Bible, since the basic work on the text of the Bible and the full notes was undertaken by French Roman Catholics at their Biblical School in Jerusalem. This basic textual preparation was the result of 50 years' study. The team of French scholars was headed by Father Roland de Vaux, one of the greatest authorities on the Dead Sea Scrolls.

The Jerusalem Bible first appeared as a French translation. This is said to be amongst the most beautiful examples of French ever to have been written. The English version (translated by a different team, including poets and writers in English) was from the same carefully prepared Hebrew and Greek texts and contains the same notes as the French version. A revision of this work was made in 1986 and is called the New Jerusalem Bible.

The New English Bible—1970

The NEB was first proposed by the Church of Scotland in 1946 and was finally jointly sponsored by all the major churches in Britain, together with the Bible Societies (which exist to promote Bible translation). Part of the instruction to the translators was that it should be, "a completely new translation . . free to employ a contemporary idiom (the way people speak today) rather than reproduce 'biblical' English." There are times when the reader feels there may have been changes for change's sake, not for the sake of accuracy but "just to be different". The limitations of this popular translation are well-expressed in the introduction to the (revised) New Testament in 1970:

> Taken as a whole, our version claims to be a translation, free, it may be, rather than literal, but a faithful translation nevertheless, so far as we could compass it.

New American Standard Bible—1971

This is a thoroughgoing revision of the American Standard Version of 1901. It is an outstanding literal translation and is used by many students throughout the world as a working Bible for study purposes.

"Good News Bible"—1976 (Today's English Version)

The American Bible Society produced a translation of the New Testament called, "Good News for Modern Man," in 1966 as the first part of a complete Bible to be known as "Today's English Version." Subsequently, parts of the Old Testament were published in separate book form as they were finished. The book of Job is one of the clearest translations of this difficult drama yet produced, whilst on the other hand the Psalms are quite disappointing. The whole Bible has now been published with helpful headings to break up the text and clean line-drawings to add impact. It is popularly known as the "Good News Bible."

The GNB reads very smoothly but tends towards paraphrase (that is, not translation of the exact words of the original language as closely as possible into English, but a re-phrasing of the English to suggest the overall meaning). Our final chapter in this Section will have more to say about the GNB and its importance for modern methods of Bible translation.

Paraphrases are useful to give the general idea of the Bible but are of little value when you start to study the Bible seriously for yourself, or in Bible study groups.

The New International Version—1978

In 1965 the New York Bible Society sponsored a fresh translation "to do for our time what the King James's Version did for its day." It is called the New International Version since scholars from all over the English-speaking world (as widely scattered as Canada and New Zealand) were involved in its production. A central "Committee on Bible Translation" was responsible for the final wording.

Revised Authorised Version—1982

Called the New King James Version in the States, this has changed the Authorised (King James) Version as little as possible. It has modernised grammar (changing 'thee' and 'thou' to 'you', for instance) and made changes in the sixteenth century wording where this has become archaic. It has also laid out the Psalms (and elsewhere) as poetry.

The Living Bible—1971

A good example of the dangers of paraphrase is the Living Bible (1971), which does not follow the original text at all faithfully, and sometimes reflects the paraphraser's religious views more clearly than those of the original writers. In Kenneth Taylor's own words in his Preface to The Living Bible.

> There are dangers in paraphrases, as well as virtues. For whenever the author's exact words are not translated from the original languages, there is a possibility that the translator, however honest may be giving the English read something that the original writer did not mean to say.

But no one would deny that The Living Bible is lively and easy to follow.

Moffat—1928

Other attempts by individuals to convey the meaning of the Old and New Testaments, that have stood the test of time, are Moffat (complete Bible 1928) and J. B. Phillips (''N.T. in modern English''—1958 and parts of the O.T. in 1963). Moffat's work was a very free, lively presentation and was one of the first to re-arrange verses in the hopes of making the text easier to follow (Jerusalem Bible and NEB also change verses around but to a lesser degree). Despite this kind of interference with the text and many instances of loose paraphrase, there are some illuminating details of translation.

J. B. Phillips—N.T. 1956

J. B. Phillips, in his preface on the art of translation, discusses this modern, less literal approach, in these words:

> We do not care if a sentence be inverted or expanded or re-arranged, so long as we are confident that a conscientious translator is faithfully conveying the meaning of his author to our minds and hearts.

His comments on Old Testament Hebrew show what Phillips can compress into few words. First, here is what Martin Luther had to say about the Hebrew language:

> The words of the Hebrew tongue have a peculiar energy. It is impossible to convey so much so briefly in any other language.

Now see how Phillips says the same thing, in one short sentence:

> In Hebrew almost every letter is a tensed muscle.

The story of twentieth century translation, is, therefore, somewhat strange. Never before has there been such a concern for accuracy of the original text of the Bible, yet, on the other hand, such a tendency towards paraphrase and "free" translation.

Why should this be? Read on!

Comparative Translations of Psalm 23:1–4

Authorised (King James) Version

The LORD is my shepherd;
I shall not want.
He maketh me to lie down in green pastures:
he leadeth me beside the still waters.
He restoreth my soul:
he leadeth me in the paths of righteousness for his name's sake.
Yea, though I walk through the valley of the shadow of death,
I will fear no evil:
for thou art with me;
thy rod and thy staff they comfort me.

New English Bible

The LORD is my shepherd;
I shall want nothing.
He makes me to lie down in green pastures,
and leads me beside the waters of peace;
he renews life within me,
and for his name's sake
guides me in the right path.
Even though I walk through a valley
dark as death, I fear no evil,
for thou art with me,
thy staff and thy crook are my comfort.

Good News Bible

The LORD is my shepherd;
I have everything I need.
He lets me rest in fields of green grass
and leads me to quiet pools of fresh water.
He gives me new strength
He guides me in right paths,
as he has promised.
Even if I go through the deepest darkness,
I will not be afraid, LORD,
for you are with me.
Your shepherd's rod and staff protect me.

The Living Bible (Paraphrase)

Because the LORD is my Shepherd,
I have everything I need!
He lets me rest in the meadow grass
and leads me beside the quiet streams.
He restores my failing health.
He helps me do what honours him the most.
Even when walking through the dark valley of death
I will not be afraid,
for you are close beside me,
guarding, guiding all the way.

PART THREE

The Bible Amongst the Nations

Problems of translation

Jesus once told the story of a Jewish tax-collector who suddenly realised how full his life was of greed and godlessness. He came to the Temple, his pride defeated, to pray; to find in God, someone who would understand and forgive. Jesus tells how he "beat his breast" in remorse (Luke 18:13). "Beat his breast"—an easy phrase to translate, you might think. After all, every language must have a word meaning "to beat" and every human being has a chest! The problem arises when you start translating the New Testament into the West Zambian language of Chokwe. For these people, "beat the chest" means to congratulate yourself, to be pleased with yourself—exactly the opposite of the feeling of the tax-collector! The only way round this problem way to say, in Chokwe, "beat his brows."

A different kind of translation problem is represented by the curious fact that in most languages of the Philippines, if you repeat a word (as we frequently do for emphasis) you give the impression of being unsure. Thus, if you translated the phrase that Jesus uses when he wants to say something of great importance, "truly, truly I say to you . . .," word for word, you would give quite the wrong idea, i.e. "I'm not quite sure about this, but . . ."

The basic problem about Bible translation, then, is that not all languages are able to convey the same ideas in the same way: in fact, the same phrase in one language ("beat the breast," for example) can have a completely opposite meaning in another language.

Before you go any further into this final chapter of the Bible's story, decide together what you think these words mean: "worry", "worship". and "thankfulness", before you read page 58.

The Bible in New Languages

In direct contrast with existing spoken languages with no written form, which were required to develop one to convey God's word for men, experiments have been made in creating new languages, starting with the written word. Esperanto, the most popular international language, is a case in point. The whole Bible has been translated into this artificial language.

The case of Afrikaans in South Africa is very different. This new language has its origins stretching back for two centuries, but its first regular appearance in writing was in a correspondence column of the Dutch language newspaper *Kaapse Grensblad* published by Louis Meurant in Grahamstown in the 1850's.

The "father of the Afrikaans language" was a medical man in the Dutch Royal Navy, Dr Arnoldus Pannevis, and it was this doctor from Holland who wrote to the British and Foreign Bible Society in 1874 proposing that a translation into the new literary language of Afrikaans be undertaken. The first translator to be commissioned was S. J. du Toit, who worked on different parts of the Bible between 1889 and 1908. As with the "Four Gospels and Psalms" (1922), the problem with all these early attempts at an Afrikaans Bible was that they were translated from the Dutch or English. It was not until 1933 that the first complete Afrikaans Bible appeared translated direct from the original languages of Hebrew and Greek. This 1933 Afrikaans version is an accurate, scholarly translation, which many translators state as one of the best translations in any language.

But even new languages change and two fresh Afrikaans versions have been published recently: one following the principles of dynamic equivalence which we are about to discuss (and making use of Today's English Version), and the other, a paraphrase based on The Living Bible.

Dynamic Equivalence

Modern translators of the Bible have worked out a very simple (but certainly not easy) method called Dynamic Equivalence. It works like this:

1. Original word/phrase (Greek or Hebrew).
2. All the *ideas* which this contains.
3. Those *ideas* translated into the other language.
4. The best word or phrase to convey the main *idea* of the original.

Let's take the example with which we opened the chapter.

1. **Original Words** (Greek, Luke 18:13)
   etypten (he beat)
   eis (on)
   to stethos (the breast)
   autou (of himself)
2. **Ideas behind those words**
   1. he was sorry for what he had done.
   2. he showed that sorrow in an action.
   3. he hit himself to prove that he wanted to punish and change himself.
   4. he hit himself over his heart (which throughout the Bible represents the understanding).
3. **These ideas are then transferred into the Chokwe language.**
4. The best natural equivalent in Chokwe becomes ''he beat his brows'' (to show a change of mind and thinking).

The translation that has followed this method most carefully, is the American Bible Society's Good News Bible (see page 50). This version is now being used as the basis for new translation into many languages of the world.

There is no Best Language

The Navajo Indian word for "worry" means "my mind is killing me." Did you come up with anything better?

The Cuicatec Indians of Mexico use what seems at first a very odd idea for "worship"; it means "to wag the tail before God." Think back to your own discussion about worship. Was any similar idea raised? The neighbouring Tzeltal tribe use a quite different phrase for worship, which speaks of "ending yourself before God." (What we would call "humbling yourself.")

For the feeling of "thankfulness" the Karree people of Central Africa have an expression, "to sit down on the ground before God." These people sit in front of the hut of a man who has helped them or been kind, just to show how much they like to be near their generous friend.

These examples illustrate the fact that each language has its own way of saying things. In English, for example, trains and noses "run"; in Afrikaans they "walk".

No language is "better" or "worse" than another. Each has its strengths. Zulu, for instance, has 120 words to describe different ways of walking. (English has only about 20—"ramble", "totter", "stride" and so on). The Swazis have a phrase to describe the dawn—"he left the darkness behind him in the house." Surely no other language on earth could describe the wonder of Luke 24:1–7 so perfectly, when Jesus left the darkness behind forever.

The Bible Societies

This reference to the Bible being translated into many languages, brings us to the incredible achievements of the Bible Societies since the first was founded in London in 1804.

It was a sixteen-year-old Welsh girl who began it all. Mary Jones wanted to read the Bible in her own language so much that she walked 40 kms (25 miles) to buy one, only to be disappointed. Too few Welsh Bibles were printed for the growing demand. Deeply touched by Mary's tears of disappointment, the local minister, Thomas Charles, gave her one of his own Bibles. But he did not leave the matter there. At the next committee meeting of the Religious Tract Society in London, Mr. Charles raised the need for a cheap Bible in Welsh. The secretary of the committee,

Joseph Hughes, made a bold suggestion: "Surely a society might be founded for the purpose, and if for Wales, why not for the Kingdom, why not for the whole world!" Thus the British and Foreign Bible Society was formed on 7 March 1804.

In the first hundred years of its existence this amazing society, which depends entirely on gifts of money from individuals and churches, had printed 180 million Bibles, New Testaments and smaller selections. By 1965 it had been responsible for the translation of the Bible (at least in part) into 677 different languages.

Soon, other Bible Societies were operating (Netherlands 1814; America 1816; South Africa 1820). Thirty-five of these societies now work together as the United Bible Societies which in 1975 alone printed 300 million Bibles and portions in 1 575 languages. Ninety seven per cent of the world's population can read some part of the Bible in their mother tongue.

But figures do not convey the sheer hard work and frequently the fearful suffering which lies behind almost every translation.

Some Famous Translators

There was William Carey, a shoemaker and repairer with the East India Company at Serampore (India). He taught himself Latin, Greek and Hebrew and was responsible for four complete translations into Indian dialects, which he completed in his first fourteen years in India. He and his companions were the first to receive help from the BFBS (British and Foreign Bible Society). In 1813 Carey was working on a translation into the tenth Indian dialect when a fire broke out in the premises where the Bibles were printed. The work of many years (not only his manuscripts of Bible translations but also of grammars and dictionaries which Carey had painstakingly produced) were totally destroyed in the blaze.

Here is what he wrote to London after the disaster:

> We are cast down, but not in despair . . . Travelling a road a second time is usually done with greater ease and certainty . . . We shall improve the translation lost!

William Carey, the shoemaker, became Professor of Bengali in the Government College at Calcutta and died in 1834 having been involved in twenty-six translations of the Bible into Indian languages and dialects.

About the same time Henry Martyn, also stationed in India, but with a brilliant university career behind him, received crushing news. Within twelve hours he heard from his girlfriend in England that she was not prepared to marry him, and his doctor confirmed that Henry was suffering from incurable tuberculosis. Only a lonely, painful death faced him. But in the six years that his sheer willpower kept him alive, he translated the New Testament into Urdu, Persian and Arabic, actually riding on horseback for a thousand miles in the process, through mountain passes and across burning deserts, eventually dying in a stable behind an inn in Turkey in 1812. Perhaps, as he lay dying, he thought of where Jesus, his Master, had been born.

The first translation into an African language is not so dramatic a story but the labours of Robert Moffat on the Southern Tswana Bible deserve our gratitude. The bare facts require our imaginations to fill them out. In 1830 Luke's Gospel; 1840 New Testament; 1843 Psalms and New Testament; 1857 complete Bible. Moffat's first task was to patiently work out a written form of a language whose grammar was totally different from his own (look back to page 43). Next came the problem of printing. Luke's Gospel was printed in Cape Town with Moffat himself setting the type by hand. In 1831 he was given a small printing press, not much quicker or easier to use than Gutenberg's of 370 years earlier. On this, much of his later published material was laboriously printed, a sheet at a time. All this while, Moffat was undertaking his normal duties as a priest in an area covering much of the Botswana of today. The story of Mary Jones was repeated many times over, with Tswana tribesmen walking 160 kms (100 miles) and more, driving sheep before them to exchange for a copy of the Gospel of Luke in their own language. Moffat's strength of character influenced great events of African history: David Livingstone ("Dr. Livingstone, I presume") was his son-in-law, and was, in fact, responsible for bringing out the first 500 Tswana New Testaments (which had been printed in London under Moffat's editorship).

This century, too, has seen its hardships and perils. In January 1956, five young missionaries to the Auca tribe of Ecuador were murdered by hostile tribesmen close to the light aircraft in which they had just arrived to begin work on a translation. The news brought horror throughout the world as it hit the headlines. Two and a half years later, the first white missionary to venture back into Auca territory was Rachel Saint, the sister of one of the murdered men. She had spent the intervening time learning the language of the tribe and working on a translation of the New Testament for the men who had killed her brother.

Perhaps these few stories are enough to show that the spirit of the early pioneer translators, such as Luther and Tyndale, is not dead. The work of translation is never ended, even in countries already well served, for revision and re-translation are continually in progress. Nor is this painstaking occupation always done "out in the bush." The author has been privileged to watch a team of translators at work on a new Zulu version in the heart of Durban. One can sense that small upper room in a concrete jungle is a power house that may influence the lives of hundreds of thousands of Zulu people in time to come. For, as a New Testament writer wrote of the Old Testament:

> **The Word of God is something alive and active.**
>
> Hebrews 4:12—Jerusalem Bible